DATE DUE

DEC 3 0 1998		
DEC 1 8 2002		
MAR 2 2 2011		

HIGHSMITH   # 45220

Sales and Distribution

Careers for Today

Sales and Distribution

Linda Barrett
Galen Guengerich

Franklin Watts

New York • London • Toronto • Sydney

Developed by: 𝛀 **Visual Education Corporation**
Princeton, NJ

Cover photograph: © Henley & Savage/The Stock Market

Photo Credits: p. 6 Bob Daemmrich; p. 11 David R. Frazier Photolibrary; p. 12 David
R. Frazier Photolibrary; p. 14 David R. Frazier Photolibrary; p. 16 Gabe Palmer/The
Stock Market; p. 20 Bob Daemmrich; p. 23 Bob Daemmrich; p. 26 Bob Daemmrich;
p. 30 Sepp Seitz/Woodfin Camp & Associates, Inc.; p. 32 David R. Frazier
Photolibrary; p. 34 George Zimbel/Monkmeyer Press; p. 38 P. Proctor/The Stock
Market; p. 41 Jeff Greenberg; p. 44 Steve Dunwell/The Image Bank; p. 47 Bob
Daemmrich; p. 50 David R. Frazier Photolibrary; p. 52 David R. Frazier Photo-
library; p. 56 Blumebild/H. Armstrong Roberts; p. 59 Dan McCoy/Rainbow; p. 62
Jeff Greenberg; p. 66 David R. Frazier Photolibrary; p. 68 David R. Frazier
Photolibrary; p. 71 Randy Matusow/Monkmeyer Press; p. 74 Mavournea Hay/
Daemmrich Photos; p. 77 Mark Dolster/International Stock Photo;
p. 80 Bob Daemmrich.

Library of Congress Cataloging-in-Publication Data

Barrett, Linda
Sales and distribution / Linda Barrett and Galen Guengerich.
p.   cm. — (Careers for today)
Includes bibliographical references (p.   ) and index.
Summary: Provides vocational guidance to those interested in retail trade careers
such as sales, marketing, and distribution. Describes wages and salaries in these
occupations and explains how to prepare résumés and conduct interviews.
ISBN 0-531-11105-9
1. Retail trade — Vocational guidance. 2. Retail trade — Vocational guidance
—United States. 3. Retail trade — United States — Job descriptions. 4. United States
—Occupations. [1. Retail trade —Vocational guidance.   2. Occupations.   3. Vocational guidance.] I. Guengerich, Galen.   II. Title. III. Series.
HF5429.29.B37   1991
658.8′7′002373 — dc20   90-12991 CIP AC

Contents

Introduction

How many things do high school students buy each month? Let's make a list of some things they might buy:

- Tickets to a movie or a ball game
- A sweater, shirt, or pair of jeans
- A card to send to a sick classmate
- A record, tape, or compact disc
- A hamburger, french fries, and a soda
- A pair of sneakers
- A gift for a friend's birthday

The list could go on and on. However, the point it makes is clear. Buying and selling are part of our way of life. If people never bought anything, their lives would be very different.

But people do buy things. They buy things someone else has made. Something needs to link the buyer with the maker or the consumer with the producer. That link is formed by sales and distribution workers. They are the bridge between producers and consumers.

This book can help high school students and graduates find out about jobs in sales and distribution. The jobs in this field are as varied as the people who will fill them. So graduates can follow their interests and abilities and find jobs that are right for them.

Sales and Distribution Today

The sales and distribution field includes a wide variety of jobs that may interest graduates: retail sales worker, supermarket worker, stock clerk, route delivery worker, direct sales worker, telemarketer, equipment rental and leasing clerk, auto sales worker, wholesale trade sales worker, advertising sales worker, and real estate sales worker.

The future looks bright for students interested in sales and distribution jobs. As the graph below shows, some jobs are growing faster than others. So it is important to look into a job carefully before making a decision.

Growth in Jobs Through the Year 2000

Little Change	Average Growth	Faster than Average Growth	Much Faster than Average Growth

stock clerk
supermarket worker
route delivery worker
advertising sales worker
retail sales worker
direct sales worker
telemarketer
equipment rental and leasing clerk
auto sales worker
wholesale trade sales worker
real estate agent

Choosing a Career in Sales and Distribution

Sales and distribution workers form a bridge between producers and consumers. But many different types of workers make up the bridge. Distribution workers move goods from the places where they are made to places where people can buy them. Here is where the sales workers take over. Their job is to persuade people to buy the goods.

Sales workers may find that some people resist buying. They learn how to overcome these objections. Sales workers should be friendly and polite. But they should be eager to persuade people to make purchases.

More than anything else, sales workers need to have enthusiasm. They must believe in the products they are selling. Sales workers should be convinced that their products are important and that people need to buy them. Successful sales workers spread their enthusiasm to their customers.

High school graduates can choose from a number of careers in sales and distribution. They may

- Sell new and used cars, trucks, and vans
- Sell newspapers, credit cards, office equipment, and other goods over the telephone
- Deliver bread, dry-cleaned clothes, and other goods to regular customers on routes
- Sell products in bulk to stores and companies

- Rent or lease equipment and other items
- Work in grocery stores or supermarkets
- Help customers and sell goods in retail stores
- Control the flow of goods in warehouses
- Sell houses, apartments, and other properties
- Sell advertising for newspapers, magazines, and radio and television stations
- Sell manufacturers' products directly to customers

People interested in these and other jobs can easily find out more about them. One way to learn is by working part-time. High school students can often work in the evening, on weekends, or during vacations. Many stores hire students to help customers or work at cash registers. Students may

- Work as cashiers in department stores
- Sell tickets to movie theater customers
- Serve delicatessen customers at convenience stores
- Stock shelves in supermarkets
- Rent videocassettes to customers at video stores
- Sell shoes to customers at shoe stores
- Help customers in sporting goods stores

Some of these jobs will help students develop sales skills. Part-time jobs can also help students decide which career is right for them. These jobs give students a head start for the future.

Today large shopping malls draw great crowds to retail shops and provide numerous jobs.

Preparing for a Career in Sales and Distribution

A large number of people have sales and distribution jobs. There are more than 13.5 million sales jobs alone. And that number will increase by more than 20 percent by the year 2000. Many new workers will be needed to fill these new jobs. More will be needed to replace workers who retire or take other jobs.

Though plenty of jobs are available, the best jobs will go to people who are prepared. People who want sales and distribution jobs should begin preparing in high school. Each job profile in this book lists courses students can take.

A stock clerk unloads a shipment of computers in the warehouse.

Many profiles list English, speech, and communications courses. Being able to communicate clearly is a key part of sales work. These courses will help students improve their communications skills. Some sales profiles list psychology courses as well. These courses teach students how people think and make decisions. Sales workers can be more effective if they know about these processes.

Business, math, and bookkeeping courses are useful for some jobs. Sales and distribution workers often need to record sales and inventory. Students should also take computer courses in data entry and data processing. Computers are used in many different ways in the sales and distribution field. Many retail stores have cash registers that are linked to central computers. Many stockrooms and warehouses use computerized inventory control systems. Most auto and real estate sales workers use computers as well. They keep lists of cars and properties for sale on a computer. Students who know how to use a computer will have an advantage when applying for jobs.

12

Some people may want to take courses beyond high school. Vocational and technical schools and community colleges offer courses to prepare people for sales and distribution careers. These courses may last from several weeks to a year.

Trends in Sales and Distribution

Scanners   Retail stores will continue to improve the way customers pay for goods. More and more stores are using scanners. These scanners read an item's Universal Product Code (UPC) label, which is a series of black lines. The item and its price are instantly recorded. This means customers can pay for their goods faster.

Inventory Control   Inventory control has become a big concern of many stores and wholesalers. A company's inventory is its stock of unsold goods. A company needs enough inventory to meet the needs of its customers. But a company must pay for the goods it has on hand. Too much inventory can reduce profits.

So many wholesalers and large retail stores are turning to "just in time" inventory systems. They order goods so that the goods arrive just in time to sell or ship to retailers. This system keeps inventories smaller and saves money. But it also means that exact inventory records are necessary. As a result, computerized inventory control is becoming more popular.

The field of sales and distribution offers many opportunities for a rewarding career. Students should look at a number of options before making a decision. That way, they can be certain the job is one that fits their abilities and interests.

Chapter 1
Retail Sales Worker

Retail sales workers help customers and sell goods in retail stores. Their jobs are as varied as the stores they work in. Some retail sales workers work in small gift shops. Others work in huge department stores. The employers of retail sales workers include

- Clothing, shoe, and department stores
- Furniture, appliance, and carpet stores
- Gift shops, hobby shops, and bookstores
- Computer, electronics, and camera stores
- Home-improvement centers

Education, Training, and Salary

Full-time retail sales workers need a high school education. Students will find some courses very helpful in preparing for sales work. These courses include English, math, and speech. Camera shops, computer stores, and other specialty stores may require sales experience. These stores may also look for sales workers who know about their products.

Retail sales workers train on the job. New workers may learn how to use cash registers when the store is closed. Or they may be taught in a classroom. Experienced workers show them how to display and price new items. New workers may also spend some time working in the stock-

15

Retail sales workers often act as cashiers.

room. That way they learn about the products the store carries.

The pay of retail sales workers varies greatly. The size of the store, the type of goods, and the experience of the worker all affect earnings. Also, some sales workers earn a commission. That means they receive a certain percentage of the price of each item they sell. New retail sales workers begin at about $10,000 a year. Overall, workers average $15,000 a year. Some experienced workers earn over $20,000 a year.

Benefits for full-time workers usually include paid vacations and holidays, health insurance, and a pension plan. Most stores give their employees a discount on goods sold in the store.

Job Description

The duties of retail sales workers depend on the stores they work in. However, in most stores sales workers have three main duties:

- Showing merchandise to customers and helping them decide what to buy
- Keeping merchandise displays attractive and well stocked
- Operating cash registers and helping customers pay for their purchases

In a paint store, sales workers show paint chips and wallpaper samples to customers. They may mix paint and order wallpaper. Sales workers in a furniture store discuss interior design with customers. They suggest which pieces of furniture go well together. They may also arrange for customers to buy the furniture on credit.

Home entertainment sales workers tell customers about the features of different televisions. They play music through several audio systems so customers can hear the differences between them. Bookstore sales workers answer questions about book titles in stock. They may place special orders for customers.

In some stores, sales workers act mainly as cashiers. This is especially true in department and variety stores. They total all the customers' purchases and take the payment. The store may accept cash, checks, credit cards, and direct debit cards. Some stores also have their own credit plans and accounts.

Retail sales workers arrange merchandise and displays. They mark prices on each item and

All the shelves have been stocked. The merchandise has been checked and priced. This afternoon we will be putting the finishing touches on the display racks. Tomorrow is the big day. The front doors will open at 10 A.M. And customers will come into our new store for the very first time.

My name is Nicole Pierce. I'm a sales worker at the new department store at the mall. Even though the store hasn't opened yet, I've been working here for a month. My first two weeks were spent in training.

My favorite part of training was learning about the cash registers. The registers are actually computer terminals. When an item is sold, the computer auto- matically subtracts it from the inventory list.

If the customer buys something with a credit card, the computer calls the credit card company for an approval. The process takes only about fifteen seconds. Computers make our whole store more efficient.

I already enjoy my job. And I think I'll like helping customers even more. I'll be working in the women's fashions department. I've been interested in clothes for as long as I can remember. People often tell me I have a good eye for fashion. That's an ability I can put to good use in my new job. My customers will benefit. And I can earn a living doing something I enjoy.

restock the displays. Sometimes they put up special displays and prices for sales.

In small stores, sales workers may help take inventory and order new stock. They may answer the telephone and speak with suppliers. Experienced sales workers may arrange for advertising for the store. Some also open and close the store.

Outlook for Jobs

People who are interested in a retail sales career can begin while in high school. Many stores hire high school students to work evenings, on weekends, or during vacation periods. Students may help customers or work at cash registers. This experience can help students develop sales skills. It will give students an advantage when looking for full-time jobs.

Retail sales workers can advance as they gain experience. They may become department supervisors or managers. Some experienced sales workers enter the management training programs of large retail chain stores. With more education, they can become store managers.

The number of retail stores continues to grow. New sales workers are needed to fill new jobs and replace people who advance or take other jobs. People who enjoy selling can look forward to a rewarding career.

For more information on retail sales workers, write to:

National Retail Merchants Association

New York, NY 10001
(212) 244–8780

United Food and Commercial Workers International Union
1775 K Street, NW
Washington, DC 20006
(202) 223–3111

Chapter 2
Supermarket Worker

Supermarket workers do a variety of jobs in grocery stores and supermarkets. Their duties include stocking shelves, cutting up meat, baking breads and pastries, serving delicatessen customers, and checking and bagging groceries.

Education, Training, and Salary

Most supermarket workers do not need to meet any educational requirements. They are trained on the job by experienced workers. However, people who want to be butchers need a high school education. Some butchers are trained by their employers on the job. Others become apprentices with a butchers' labor union. It takes two to three years to become a fully trained butcher.

The pay of supermarket workers depends on their experience. New workers earn about $10,000 a year. Overall, supermarket workers average $15,000 a year. Supervisors earn an average of $20,000 a year. Experienced butchers who belong to a labor union earn up to $30,000 a year. Benefits for full-time workers usually include paid vacations and holidays, health insurance, and a pension plan.

Job Description

Everyone needs to eat. For most people, eating is also a pleasure. Supermarket workers help make available a wide variety of foods that people can enjoy. The duties of supermarket workers depend on their jobs. There are seven main jobs in a supermarket. In small stores, each worker may do several of these jobs.

Stock Clerk   Stock clerks receive shipments of goods sent to the store. They check the shipping invoice to make sure the shipment is correct. Then they place the items in the storeroom.

As customers empty the shelves, stock clerks put new goods in place. The manager may tell them to expand or reduce the space for a certain item. Clerks also change displays for sales or special promotions.

In some stores, clerks place a price stamp on each item. However, more and more supermarkets are using automatic scanners at the checkout counters. These stores must still place price markers on the shelves under each item.

Clerks may regularly count the items in stock. Managers need this information to order new supplies. Some experienced stock clerks may help place the orders. Stock clerks also keep shelves and displays tidy and answer customers' questions. Some stock clerks check and bag groceries.

Delicatessen Clerk   Deli clerks take orders from customers for deli items. These include sliced meats and cheeses, salads, and foods prepared in the store. Many deli items are ordered and priced by the pound. Clerks weigh the or-

A delicatessen clerk slices meat for a customer.

ders, wrap them, and place price labels on the packages. They keep the deli display clean and filled with food. Deli clerks sometimes wrap items for sale in the self-service areas of the store.

Bakery Clerk Some supermarkets buy their baked goods from outside bakeries. In other supermarkets, bakery clerks bake bread, cakes, pies, cookies, and other pastries. In all supermarkets, bakery clerks place baked goods in boxes or bags. Then they put them in display cases. The clerks also help customers with bakery items.

Butcher Butchers cut up large pieces of beef, pork, and veal into roasts, steaks, chops, and other cuts. Some of the meat is put through a meat grinder. Wrappers package the various cuts of meat and then mark and price them. The meat is placed in a display counter for customers to buy. Most butchers cut up poultry as well. Butchers often answer customers' questions about cuts of meat and how to cook them. They also fill special orders for cuts of meat.

23

There are more than 235,000 retail food stores in the United States. About 165,000 of these stores are grocery stores, and 27,000 are large supermarkets. The rest are convenience stores and specialty food shops.

One of the first supermarkets was built in New York City in 1930. The idea spread quickly. By 1932, there were eight supermarkets. One was in an old car factory in Elizabeth, New Jersey.

Today, only about 11 percent of all food stores in the United States are supermarkets. But supermarkets account for almost 70 percent of food store sales.

Produce Clerk   Produce clerks take care of the supermarket's fruits and vegetables. They make sure the temperature and humidity in the storeroom are correct. Often, clerks package some of the items. Then they place fruits and vegetables in display cases. To keep the cases neat and attractive, clerks remove wilted leaves or produce from the display. They may also spray water on the produce to keep it fresh.

Checker   Checkers operate the supermarket's cash registers. In some stores, checkers pass the groceries over an automatic scanner. They may weigh some produce and deli items. Checkers total the customers' orders, subtracting the value of coupons. Checkers take the customers' payments. The store may accept cash, checks, credit cards, and direct debit cards. Checkers may also help bag the groceries.

Bagger   Baggers place each customer's groceries in paper or plastic bags. Sometimes, baggers take the groceries to the customers' cars.

24

Outlook for Jobs

People interested in supermarket jobs can begin while in high school. Many supermarkets hire students part-time. The students may work as baggers or checkers, or stock, deli, or bakery clerks. This can help students gain experience.

Supermarket workers can advance as they gain experience. Workers can become supervisors or department managers. With more training and education, department managers can become assistant managers or store managers. Most store managers have college degrees.

People who want to be supermarket workers have a promising future. Computers and automation will affect the way some jobs are done. However, a growing population will increase the need for supermarket workers. There will continue to be many new jobs in the future.

For more information on supermarket workers, write to:

American Meat Institute
1700 North Moore Street, Suite 1600
Arlington, VA 22209
(703) 841–2400

National Grocers Association
1825 Samuel Morris Drive
Reston, VA 22090–5317
(703) 437–5300

United Food and Commercial Workers International Union
1775 K Street, NW
Washington, DC 20006
(202) 223–3111

Chapter 3
Stock Clerk

Stock clerks work in wholesale warehouses and retail storerooms. They control the flow of goods and keep inventory records. In warehouses, clerks receive goods from manufacturers, store them until they are needed, and then ship them to retailers. Some warehouses divide these jobs among stock clerks, shipping clerks, and receiving clerks.

In storerooms, clerks store goods received from wholesalers and manufacturers until the goods are needed. Then they send them to the retail sales floor. Clerks also stock shelves and displays.

Education, Training, and Salary

There are no educational requirements for stock clerks. However, many employers prefer to hire people with a high school education. While in high school, students should take courses in math, data entry, data processing, typing, business, and English. These courses will make it easier to learn the job.

Stock clerks are trained on the job by experienced clerks. New clerks begin by unloading shipments of goods. They learn where each item is stored in the warehouse or storeroom. They also learn how to operate power lifts, use inventory scanners, and keep records.

New stock clerks earn an average of $9,000 a year. Experienced clerks may earn up to $15,000 a year. Benefits usually include paid vacations and holidays, health insurance, and a pension plan.

Job Description

Stock Clerk   Stock clerks take care of a company's stock (supply of goods). They unpack the goods when they arrive from a manufacturer or wholesaler. The goods must be checked against the invoice to make sure everything is there. If an item is damaged, it is sent back. Clerks make a record of the goods received. Then they arrange the goods on shelves or in bins. Clerks may use forklift trucks to move heavy or bulky items.

When goods are needed, clerks take them out of storage. They record the number of goods removed. Wholesale stock clerks ship the goods to a retail store. Retail storeroom clerks take them to the sales floor.

Keeping accurate records of inventory is a key duty of stock clerks. A company should have enough stock to make sure it can meet its customers' needs. But too much stock can hurt profits. Stock clerks keep records and count inventory regularly. With this information, managers can decide when to order new stock.

Some warehouses use automatic equipment to move goods from one area to another. They may also use computerized inventory control systems. These systems use hand-held scanners to read bar codes on each item or box. Each scanner sends its information to a central computer. The

INVENTORY STOCK REPORT							
BRUCE BRATTA CLOTHING		STORE NO. 04					MONTH 02/92
DEPT. 05: MEN'S HOSIERY							
STOCK NO.	DESCRIPTION	COLOR	OLD BALANCE	QUANTITY SOLD	QUANTITY RECEIVED	BALANCE ON HAND	
1001	WOOL LONG	GRY	5465	2502		2963	
1002	WOOL LONG	BLU	4721	2063		2658	
1003	WOOL LONG	BLK	3650	2102	1000	2548	
1004	WOOL LONG	BRN	3924	1812		2112	
1101	WOOL ANKLE	GRY	4013	2313	800	2500	
1102	WOOL ANKLE	BLU	3729	1851	200	2078	
1103	WOOL ANKLE	BLK	4121	2227	500	2394	
1104	WOOL ANKLE	BRN	3153	1565		1588	
1203	CASHMERE ARGYLE	RED	1675	812		863	

A computerized inventory report

computer gives managers quick and accurate inventory reports.

Receiving Clerk   Receiving clerks work for wholesalers and large retailers. They receive goods arriving at the warehouse or store. They unload the shipment and check for damage. If the shipment is not complete, the clerks may trace the missing items. The clerks update the inventory records. Then they move the items to the correct place in the warehouse.

Shipping Clerk   Shipping clerks work mainly for wholesalers. They prepare goods for shipping to retail outlets and other customers. When an order arrives, the clerks collect the various items. They check to make sure the shipment is complete. Some items may need protective packaging before they are shipped. Clerks may write delivery orders for the truck drivers. They may also help load the trucks.

A stock clerk using a computerized inventory control system

Outlook for Jobs

People who are interested in becoming stock clerks can begin while in high school. Many companies hire part-time stock clerks. These clerks often work evenings, on weekends, or during vacations. Clerks who have some experience will be further ahead when looking for full-time jobs.

Stock clerks can advance as they gain experience. Some clerks take jobs with larger companies. Experienced clerks can also become invoice clerks, stock control clerks, and warehouse or stockroom supervisors.

The outlook for stock clerks is fair. The number of goods that companies ship and store continues to increase. But advances in technology allow fewer workers to handle more goods. As a result, the demand for new stock clerks will not grow as fast as the volume of goods they handle will grow. However, new stock clerks will be needed to replace workers who retire or take other jobs.

For more information on stock clerks, write to:

American Society of Transportation and Logistics
P.O. Box 33095
Louisville, KY 40232–3095
(502) 451–8150

International Brotherhood of Teamsters, Chauffeurs, Warehousemen, and Helpers of America
25 Louisiana Avenue, NW
Washington, DC 20001
(202) 624–6800

United Food and Commercial Workers International Union
1775 K Street, NW
Washington, DC 20006
(202) 223–3111

Chapter 4
Route Delivery Worker

Route delivery workers drive delivery trucks and vans. They take goods and services to regular customers. Retail drivers deliver to private homes and apartments. Wholesale drivers deliver to stores. Route delivery workers deliver items that include

- Bread, cakes, and other bakery products
- Ice
- Mineral and spring water
- Dry-cleaning and laundry items
- Diapers
- Milk, ice cream, and other dairy products
- Newspapers
- Soda, beer, wine, or liquor

Education, Training, and Salary

Route delivery workers need a high school education. While in school, they should take courses in bookkeeping, business, math, speech, and driver's education. These courses will make it easier to learn the job.

Most states require a delivery worker to have a chauffeur's license. This license allows a person to be paid for driving a vehicle. You must pass a written exam and a driving test to receive the license.

33

A route delivery worker delivering bread to a regular customer

The duties of route delivery workers may vary depending on the products or services they sell. However, many of their duties are the same. Workers may do some or all of the following:

- Load their vehicles with goods they will need
- Deliver the goods to the houses or businesses on their routes
- Place goods on store shelves
- Tell customers about special promotions and new products
- Collect money or issue invoices for the goods
- Take orders for the next delivery day
- Pick up empty packages, soiled clothes, or surplus stock
- Enter sales and deliveries in record books
- Call on possible new customers on their routes

Employers provide on-the-job training for new route delivery workers. Workers learn how to make sales and keep records. They learn about the vehicles they will be driving. Some employers give advanced driving instruction as well.

Route delivery workers begin working by helping experienced workers. After several weeks, the new workers are assigned a route. A supervisor or experienced worker goes along at first. Then the new workers are on their own.

Some companies require route delivery workers to be at least twenty-five years old. In these companies, people often begin by working in the warehouse. There they learn about the company and its products. When they turn twenty-five, they are ready to work as route delivery workers.

The pay of route delivery workers varies widely. Wholesale workers usually earn more than retail workers earn. Also, most workers are paid a minimum salary plus a commission (a percentage of their sales). Route delivery workers begin at an average of $18,000 a year. The average pay of experienced workers is $25,000 a year. Some workers earn over $30,000 a year. Benefits may include paid vacations and holidays, health insurance, and a pension plan. Workers may also receive uniforms to wear.

Job Description

Route delivery workers deliver goods to their customers. But they are not just delivery workers. Rather, they have a route of established customers These workers learn to know the customers and their needs. They try to sell them as many goods and services as they can.

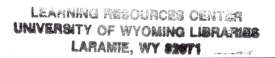

I've been working a lot of overtime lately. Don't get me wrong: I'm glad for the extra money. But I can't believe how fast business is growing. Just today my boss said she's looking for three more drivers!

My name is Tom Lee. I deliver diapers for a diaper service. Why is the diaper business taking off like a rocket? The answer is the environment.

Diaper services have been around for about sixty years. But when disposable diapers came out in 1961, many people stopped using cloth diapers. By 1990, disposables made up 85 percent of diaper industry sales.

Disposable diapers have one main benefit. It is the same as their main drawback: They are meant to be thrown way. But landfills where diapers and other trash are buried are getting full.

So people by the thousands are coming back to cloth. Cloth diapers cost less than disposables cost, and they don't fill up our landfills. We deliver four times as many diapers today as we did a year ago. That's why I'm earning extra money working overtime.

Some route delivery workers have assistants. These assistants may drive the vehicle sometimes. They may also help load and unload the goods.

Outlook for Jobs

People who are interested in route delivery work can get a head start while in high school. Many stores hire high school students to work evenings, on weekends, or during vacation periods. Students may help customers or work at cash registers. This experience can help them develop sales skills.

Students may also gain experience at delivery work. Many newspapers hire students to deliver their daily and Sunday editions. Some newspaper delivery jobs involve early-morning work. Other newspapers are delivered in the afternoon.

Route delivery workers can advance as they gain experience. Workers may move from retail to wholesale work. A few may become route supervisors or sales supervisors. Route delivery workers may also move into other sales jobs.

Overall, the outlook is good for route delivery workers. Wholesale workers may need to do less sales work in the future. More and more stores are ordering products by telephone or computer. However, route delivery drivers will still be needed to deliver the products. People interested in route delivery work can look forward to a rewarding career.

For more information on route delivery workers, write to:

American Trucking Association
2200 Mill Road
Alexandria, VA 22314
(703) 838–1700

**International Brotherhood of Teamsters,
  Chauffeurs, Warehousemen,
  and Helpers of America**
25 Louisiana Avenue, NW
Washington, DC 20001
(202) 624–6800

Chapter 5
Direct Sales Worker

Direct sales workers sell manufacturers' products directly to customers. They present these products to individuals, families, and groups. The goods they sell include

- Kitchen and household items
- Clothing, jewelry, cosmetics, or luggage
- Educational toys and games for children
- Encyclopedias and other reference books

Most direct sales workers are self-employed. As a result, they have flexible work schedules. They can also work with more than one manufacturer.

Education, Training, and Salary

Direct sales workers do not need to meet any educational requirements. However, many manufacturers prefer sales workers who have a high school education. Sales workers will find certain high school courses useful. These courses include English, math, and speech.

Most direct sales workers receive training when they begin work. They learn about the products they will be selling. They also learn sales techniques. Often new sales workers go along with experienced workers to appointments. They see how sales are made. Sometimes experienced workers help new workers with their first few sales calls.

Direct sales workers earn a commission on their sales. That means they keep a percentage of the money they receive for goods. Their income depends entirely on how much they sell. People who work full-time usually sell more than those who do not. Direct sales workers who sell through home parties can earn up to $100 per party. If they give three parties a week, they may earn up to $15,000 a year. However, they must also spend time finding people willing to have the parties. Direct sales workers provide their own benefits.

Job Description

Direct sales workers do not rely on expensive advertising campaigns. They do not need large stores or fancy showrooms. Rather, they take their products directly to possible customers, usually in customers' homes. And there, often one on one, they try to get the customers to buy.

Direct sales workers find that some people resist buying things. Sales workers learn how to overcome these objections. Sales workers should be friendly and polite at all times. But they also must be eager to persuade people to make purchases.

Before direct sales workers can sell anything, they must find possible customers. In the past, workers would go from house to house. Today, they usually contact people by telephone and make appointments. Some sales workers call or mail a letter to each home in a community.

Some direct sales workers sell through home party plans. People agree to host a party and invite their friends. In return, the host usually

Some direct sales workers sell from colorful booths in shopping malls.

receives special gifts or discounts. Party guests who agree to host a party at a later date also receive special gifts. Sales workers also set up booths in local malls or shopping centers. People who stop at the booths get information about the products. The sales workers try to persuade them to host home parties.

At parties or other appointments, direct sales workers show their goods to people. They describe the benefits of buying the products. They may show how to use toys and household items. Some clothing sales workers arrange fashion shows. Customers can try cosmetics and other personal-care items. Sales workers use many different methods. But all have the same goal: selling products to people.

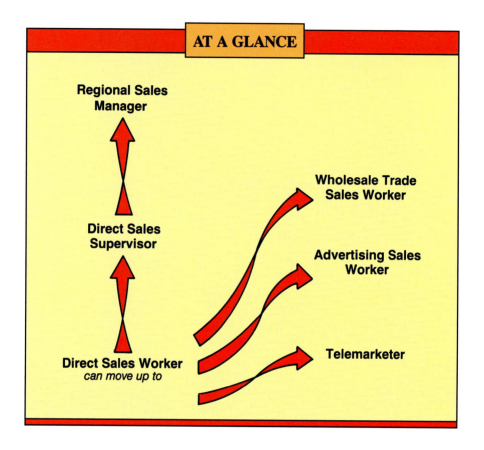

Regional Sales
Manager

Direct Sales
Supervisor

Direct Sales Worker
can move up to

Wholesale Trade
Sales Worker

Advertising Sales
Worker

Telemarketer

When people place orders, sales workers arrange for delivery of the products. Some take goods to customers and accept their payments. Sales workers pay part of the money to the manufacturer. They keep their commissions. Keeping good records is an important part of sales workers' jobs.

Outlook for Jobs

People interested in direct sales can begin preparing while in high school. Two types of experience can be helpful. Many stores hire high school students to work evenings, on weekends, or during vacation periods. Students may help customers or work at cash registers. This experience can help students develop sales skills.

Many students have opportunities to see if they enjoy direct sales. A number of clubs and school groups raise money through direct sales programs. They may sell candy, magazine subscriptions, or light bulbs.

Successful direct sales workers can advance as their sales increase. Some become supervisors of other direct sales workers. They may also become regional sales managers for manufacturers involved in direct sales. Others move into retail sales and marketing jobs.

Some experts thought home shopping channels on television would cause a decline in direct sales. That has not happened. The demand for direct sales workers continues to grow. Many direct sales workers work either part-time or for short periods between other jobs. Yet those who enter direct sales can find it a flexible and money-making job.

For more information on direct sales workers, write to:

American Marketing Association
250 South Wacker Drive, Suite 200
Chicago, IL 60606–5819
(312) 648–0536

Direct Selling Association
1776 K Street, NW
Washington, DC 20006
(202) 293–5760

Chapter 6
Telemarketer

Telemarketers sell goods and services over the telephone. The items they sell include

- Subscriptions to magazines and newspapers
- Credit cards, insurance, and other financial services
- Office equipment and supplies

Telemarketers may work directly for companies offering goods or services. Or they may work for agencies. Telemarketing agencies represent many different companies. Some agencies specialize in one type of item, such as credit cards. Others sell a wide variety of items. Telemarketers may work in a central office with many other telemarketers. However, some make calls from their own homes.

Education, Training, and Salary

Telemarketers do not need to meet any educational requirements. However, many employers prefer to hire people with a high school education. Telemarketers who sell certain items, such as financial services, may need a college education. Future telemarketers can take useful courses while in high school. These include speech, English, business, communications, and psychology.

Telemarketers receive on-the-job training. In most cases, an instructor teaches them about the job. New telemarketers learn how to use the telephone equipment. In some offices, the telephones are linked to computer terminals. Telemarketers also practice sales techniques and communication skills. They practice the scripts of the sales speeches they will give.

Telemarketers may get hourly wages or a commission on their sales. That means they get a certain percentage of the price of each item they sell. Their pay depends on what type of company they work for and how many hours they work. Many telemarketers work part-time. People who sell to businesses usually earn more than do those who sell to individuals.

Most telemarketers earn between $4 and $10 an hour. Those who sell to businesses may earn up to $20 an hour. Full-time telemarketers may receive paid vacations and holidays, health insurance, and a pension plan. Part-time workers and those who work at home usually provide their own benefits.

Job Description

Telemarketers are usually given lists of people or company purchasing agents to call. These people have been identified as possible customers. They may have

- Sent a card or letter asking for information about the product or service
- Bought items from the firm in the past
- Called a toll-free number in response to an advertisement

Some telemarketers work from their own homes.

- Bought similar items from other companies

Telemarketers explain the product or service to the customers. They try to persuade the customers to buy. If customers place orders, the telemarketers record them. They may describe other products and services that are available.

Telemarketers find that some people resist buying things over the telephone. They learn how to overcome these objections. Telemarketers should be friendly and polite at all times. But they also must be eager to persuade people to make purchases.

TALKING ABOUT THE JOB

My name is Katie Adams, and I'm a big fan of newspapers. That's one reason I'm a telemarketer for the *Times Express*. Think about it: Where else can you find all these things in one place:

- Interesting stories about events around the world
- Comics and crossword puzzles
- Baseball box scores
- Business news and stock market quotes
- Cooking tips and recipes
- Advice on personal matters

You get all of this in a package you can stuff in your book bag or under your arm. It won't blow a tube or run out of batteries. You get a new one delivered to your door every morning. And it costs less than a candy bar. How's that for a deal!

When I call people, I tell them what they are missing if they don't get a newspaper. Many people agree with me. They ask me to sign them up for a subscription. So I send their orders to the circulation department. In a few days, they too will enjoy the best news value in town.

My boss says he likes my enthusiasm. He thinks that's why I'm so good at what I do. I suppose he's right. But it's easy to be enthusiastic about something you believe in.

Some telemarketers collect information for manufacturers. They call people and ask them questions:

- Would you buy this item if it were available?
- How much do you think it should cost?
- How should it be packaged?
- Where have you seen advertisements for similar products?
- Which of these products would you buy?

48

The telemarketers record the answers. The answers are added up and given to the manufacturers. The information helps the manufacturers decide whether to make new products. It can also help them decide how to advertise and market products.

Outlook for Jobs

People who are interested in telemarketing can get a head start while in high school. Many stores hire high school students to work evenings, on weekends, or during vacation periods. This experience can help workers develop sales skills.

Telemarketers can advance as they gain skill and experience. Experienced workers may become supervisors or telemarketing instructors. They may also take sales or marketing jobs with large companies.

Telemarketing has become an excellent way to sell many different goods and services. More and more companies are using this sales method. As a result, the demand for telemarketers will grow rapidly in the future.

For more information on telemarketers, write to:

American Marketing Association
250 South Wacker Drive, Suite 200
Chicago, IL 60606–5819
(312) 648–0536

Direct Marketing Association
6 East Forty-third Street
New York, NY 10017
(212) 689–4977

Chapter 7
Equipment Rental and Leasing Clerk

Equipment rental and leasing clerks work for stores that rent or lease items to people and companies. These items are things people want to use for a period of time but not buy. People may rent a videocassette for a day. Or a company may lease a construction crane for a year.

Education, Training, and Salary

There are no educational requirements for rental and leasing clerks. However, many employers prefer to hire people with a high school education. While in high school, students should take courses in math, computer science, business, and English. These courses will make it easier to learn the job.

Rental and leasing clerks train on the job. New clerks learn about the items available for rent or lease. They may learn how to operate tools, cameras, computers, and other equipment. Customers often ask how to use the items they rent. Clerks learn to give clear instructions. They also learn how to fill out rental agreements and keep records.

Equipment rental and leasing clerks earn an average of $17,500 a year. Benefits usually include paid vacations and holidays, health insurance, and a pension plan.

Job Description

What can people do when they need thirty chairs for a dinner party? Or a tuxedo for the prom? Or a sailboat for an afternoon? The people could buy these items, of course. But they are expensive and may not be worth the cost if used only a few times.

Many people are choosing another solution: renting or leasing the items. That way, they can have what they need for only a fraction of the cost

This equipment rental clerk helps a family start out in their rented paddleboat.

Equipment rental and leasing is a booming industry. From 1980 to 1986, the number of stores grew from 12,000 to 26,000—more than double! And the number of employees almost doubled, rising from 115,000 to 222,000. Equipment rental and leasing clerks earn a total of more than $4 billion a year. The field offers a promising career for the future.

of buying it. People can rent or lease a wide variety of items. These include

- Construction tools and equipment
- Boats, bicycles, skis, and tents
- Videocassettes
- Gowns, tuxedos, and other formal apparel
- Farm and garden machinery
- Party supplies
- Medical equipment
- Electronic sound and audio equipment
- Moving equipment

Some stores specialize in one item, such as videocassettes. Others offer many different items to their customers.

Equipment rental and leasing clerks help customers who call or come into a store. The customers may want to see if certain items are available. They may also ask how much the rental will cost. The clerks check the inventory and give the rental or lease rate.

When a customer decides to rent an item, the clerk fills out a rental agreement. The clerk asks the customer to sign the agreement and pay a deposit. The clerk also collects the rental fee.

53

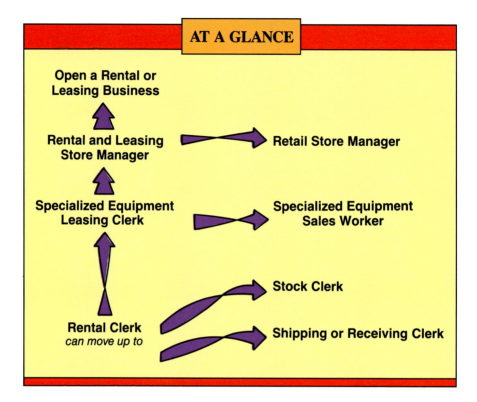

Open a Rental or Leasing Business

Rental and Leasing Store Manager → **Retail Store Manager**

Specialized Equipment Leasing Clerk → **Specialized Equipment Sales Worker**

→ **Stock Clerk**

Rental Clerk
can move up to → **Shipping or Receiving Clerk**

Then the clerk brings the item to the customer. Some large items are delivered to customers' houses or places of business.

At the end of the rental or lease period, the equipment is returned. The clerk checks to make sure it is in good condition. Then the clerk refunds the customer's deposit. He or she may prepare a final bill for the customer. Some items may have to be serviced between rentals.

Sometimes clerks mail brochures or fliers to past customers. These may describe new items or special rates. People who have their own rental and leasing businesses have other duties as well. They pay bills and keep records. They also buy new equipment and hire employees.

Outlook for Jobs

People who are interested in a career in rental and leasing can begin while in high school. Some rental stores hire high school students to work evenings, on weekends, or during vacation periods. Students may help customers or work at cash registers. This experience will give students an advantage when looking for full-time jobs.

Rental and leasing clerks can advance as they gain experience. They may become supervisors or store managers. They may also move to larger companies. Some are able to open their own rental or leasing businesses.

The future looks bright for equipment rental and leasing clerks. The cost of buying equipment is constantly increasing. People cannot always afford to buy the latest models of high-technology equipment. As a result, they rent or lease the items instead. More clerks will be needed to work in this growing market. Equipment rental and leasing clerks will find their services in demand.

For more information on rental and leasing clerks, write to:

American Association of Equipment Lessors
1300 North Seventeenth Street, Suite 1010
Arlington, VA 22209
(703) 527–8655

International Brotherhood of Teamsters,
  Chauffeurs, Warehousemen, and Helpers of
  America
25 Louisiana Avenue, NW
Washington, DC 20001
(202) 624–6800

Chapter 8
Auto Sales Worker

Auto sales workers sell new and used cars, trucks, and vans. They usually work for automobile dealers.

Education, Training, and Salary

Auto sales workers do not need to meet any educational requirements. However, many employers prefer to hire people with a high school education. Students interested in auto sales will find some high school courses especially useful. These include business, English, speech, and math.

Classes in computer science and psychology are also helpful. Many car dealerships use computers to order cars from manufacturers. Some have computerized customer and inventory records as well. Psychology tries to explain how people think and make decisions. Sales workers can be more effective if they know about these processes.

Auto sales workers train on the job. Large dealerships often have classroom training for new sales workers. These programs may be run by the dealer or by a manufacturer. They last from several days to two weeks. At other dealers, experienced sales workers train new workers.

Most auto sales workers are paid by commission. That means they receive a certain percentage of the price of each car they sell. Some sales workers are paid a small salary in addition to the commission. However, the pay of almost all auto sales workers depends on how many cars and trucks they sell.

As a result, the pay varies greatly. Auto sales workers earn an average of $24,000 a year. Some earn $50,000 or more a year. Benefits may include paid vacations and holidays, health insurance, and a pension plan. They may also have free use of cars. Most auto sales workers can buy cars at a discounted price.

Job Description

Americans buy more than 11 million new cars and trucks each year. These vehicles come in many styles and models. Some are small, fast, and sporty; others can carry a family of eight with room to spare. Most cost less than $20,000; a few cost over $100,000.

Auto sales workers try to persuade people to buy cars and trucks. They keep lists of possible customers. These customers may have answered a newspaper advertisement or called for information about a car. Sales workers keep in touch, suggest other models, and describe new features.

When people come to an auto showroom, they are usually met by a sales worker. First, the sales worker needs to find out what the customers want. Sometimes the customers have a specific car in mind. If not, the sales worker asks questions to find out what they want. Do they prefer

- A full-size, midsize, or compact car?
- A two-door coupe, four-door sedan, or station wagon?

Many auto sales workers find employment in large dealerships.

- An automatic or manual transmission?
- A four-, six-, or eight-cylinder engine?

The customers may just want to look around. Or they may want to discuss various options with the sales worker.

Once the sales worker knows the customers' preferences, he or she may suggest a test drive. The sales worker selects a car as close as possible to what the customers want and takes the customers for a short ride. The sales worker points out the car's features and performance. Available options may be suggested by the sales worker. These may include leather seats, metallic paint, an upgraded sound system, or a sunroof.

Some customers want to trade in an old car. If so, the sales worker looks at the car. He or she looks up that car model in a used-car book to figure out its value. Then the sales worker can subtract the trade-in amount from the price for the car the customers want to buy. As they do this, they try to persuade the customers to buy optional features. They may also try to sell an extended service plan.

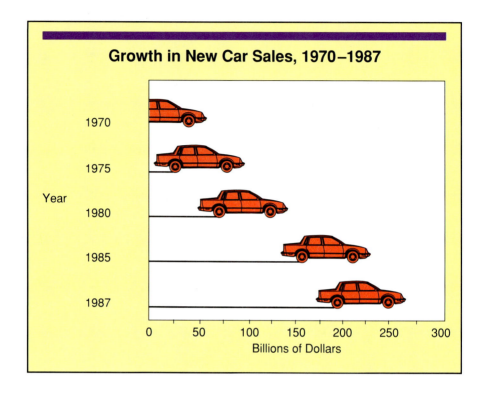

Growth in New Car Sales, 1970–1987

Year

1970
1975
1980
1985
1987

0   50   100   150   200   250   300

Billions of Dollars

Some customers already have the money to pay for the car. Others borrow money from a bank. However, more and more customers are financing cars through the dealer. Sales workers may help customers fill out a credit application. Or they may take customers to talk to the dealer's financing specialists.

Outlook for Jobs

People who are interested in an auto sales career can begin while in high school. Many stores hire high school students to work evenings, on weekends, or during vacation periods. This experience can help the workers develop sales skills. Some

60

car dealerships require sales workers to be twenty-one years old. If so, high school graduates can usually work in other departments until they are twenty-one.

Auto sales workers can advance as they gain skill in selling cars and trucks. Most successful sales workers remain in sales. They enjoy working with people. They like the challenge of persuading people to buy something. Some auto sales workers become sales managers for large dealerships. Others may open their own dealerships. Auto sales workers can also specialize in financing or leasing.

The outlook for auto sales workers is bright. The demand for new and used cars and trucks continues to increase. More dealerships will mean more jobs for sales workers. New car sales decrease during periods of slow economic growth. However, more people choose to buy used cars during these times.

For more information on auto sales workers, write to:

American Automotive Leasing Association
1001 Connecticut Avenue, NW, Suite 1201
Washington, DC 20036
(202) 223–2600

National Automobile Dealers Association
8400 Westpark Drive
McLean, VA 22102
(703) 821–7000

Chapter 9
Wholesale Trade
Sales Worker

Wholesale trade sales workers are employed by wholesalers. They sell wholesale goods in bulk to retail stores. They also sell to businesses and industrial companies.

Education, Training, and Salary

Wholesale trade sales workers need a high school education. While in school, students should take courses in bookkeeping, English, business, math, and economics. Some students may want to study economics, sales, and marketing at a junior college. These courses will prepare students to do the job well.

Manufacturers of some goods may require workers to have specialized training. Companies that make engineering equipment may look for sales workers with college training in physics and math. College classes in chemistry or biology may be required by drug or medical companies.

Job experience can also be useful. For example, construction experience is useful for wholesale building supplies sales workers. Knowledge of auto mechanics is helpful to wholesale auto parts sales workers.

Wholesale trade sales workers train on the job. Employers teach new sales workers about their products. They also describe sales techniques. New workers often go on sales calls with experienced sales workers. Training can last from a few weeks to several years. When sales workers are fully trained, they are given their own sales regions.

The pay of wholesale trade sales workers varies. A few workers receive all their pay in the form of salaries. Most get small salaries plus a commission (a percentage of their sales). A few receive only a commission. Overall, wholesale trade sales workers earn between $23,000 and $25,000 a year. However, some earn less than $20,000 a year. Some earn more than $40,000. Employers may give sales workers an advance on future commissions during slow sales periods.

Benefits usually include paid vacations and holidays, health insurance, and a pension plan. Many workers are given the use of a car and money for travel expenses. They also receive money to pay for food, hotels, and other expenses while they are traveling.

Job Description

Most manufacturers do not sell their products directly to consumers. Rather, manufacturers' representatives sell the products to large wholesale companies. Wholesale trade sales workers work for these wholesale companies. They sell products to retail stores, businesses, and large institutions.

A wholesaler usually stocks goods from a number of manufacturers. For example, a wholesaler may carry books published by fifteen different companies. So a bookstore can order books

Where Workers in the Wholesale Trade Are Employed

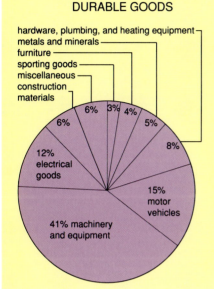

DURABLE GOODS

hardware, plumbing, and heating equipment
metals and minerals
furniture
sporting goods
miscellaneous
construction materials

6% 3% 4%
6% 5%
8%
12% electrical goods
15% motor vehicles
41% machinery and equipment

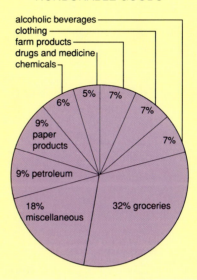

NONDURABLE GOODS

alcoholic beverages
clothing
farm products
drugs and medicine
chemicals

5% 7%
6% 7%
9% paper products
7%
9% petroleum
18% miscellaneous
32% groceries

from all these companies through one wholesaler.

Wholesale trade sales workers sell many different types of products. They include

- Equipment, supplies, and food for hotels, restaurants, hospitals, and schools
- Food for supermarkets and other retail stores
- Books, clothing, and building supplies
- China, furniture, and sporting goods
- Televisions and audio equipment
- Hardware, office supplies, and computers

Each wholesale trade sales worker is given a geographic area. Workers visit current and po-

This wholesale trade sales worker consults a map to locate some new customers in his area.

tential customers in this area. They take catalogs and samples to show buyers. They describe or demonstrate the products. If buyers have ordered before, sales workers may suggest additional items. They tell buyers about special promotions and new products.

Wholesale trade sales workers also figure prices for the buyers. Often they offer discounts for large orders or early payment. Some sales workers arrange credit accounts for new customers. They may also accept payment for the order.

The sales workers keep a record of customers' orders. The wholesaler's shipping and billing departments get copies of the orders. Workers follow up to make sure the goods arrive on time. They may also help the store with displays and advertising.

Most wholesale trade sales workers have other duties as well. They write regular reports about their sales and expenses. They keep their customer information up to date. Most wholesalers have sales meetings for their sales workers. They may also send them to conventions. There they learn about new products and sales techniques.

Outlook for Jobs

People who are interested in wholesale trade sales work can get a head start while in high school. Many stores hire high school students to work evenings, on weekends, or during vacation periods. Students may help customers or work cash registers. This experience can help them develop sales skills.

Wholesale trade sales workers can advance as they gain experience. They may become

- Wholesale sales supervisors or managers
- District sales managers
- Wholesale sales training managers

Some sales workers also take jobs in buying, advertising, or marketing.

The demand for wholesale trade sales workers will continue to increase in the future. Manufacturers are making more and more new products available. Wholesale trade sales workers will be needed to sell these products to retail stores and businesses. People who enjoy sales can look forward to rewarding careers as wholesale trade sales workers.

For more information on wholesale trade sales workers, write to:

National Association of Wholesale Distributors
1725 K Street, NW, Suite 710
Washington, DC 20006
(202) 872–0885

Sales and Marketing Executives, International
Statler Office Tower, Suite 458
Cleveland, OH 44115
(216) 771–6650

Chapter 10
Advertising
Sales Worker

Advertising sales workers sell advertising space for newspapers and magazines. They also sell advertising time for radio and television stations. A few work for companies that place outdoor advertisements on billboards, benches, buses, and taxis.

Education, Training, and Salary

Advertising sales workers need a high school education. Employers prefer students who have taken high school courses in English, math, economics, speech, and statistics. Some large employers may require college training. These include national magazines and radio and television stations in major cities.

Advertising sales workers train on the job. New workers must learn about the audiences their publications or stations reach. Much of their selling is done by telephone. Sales workers learn how to make calls and sell advertisements. They learn about advertising rates and details. New workers also travel with experienced sales workers to meet with customers at their offices.

The pay of advertising sales workers depends on the size of their employers. Some workers are paid salaries. Others also get a commission (a percentage of the price of each ad they sell). New

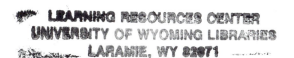

advertising sales workers earn between $16,000 and $19,000 a year. Experienced workers average between $24,000 and $30,000 a year. Those at large companies in major cities may earn more than $40,000. Sales workers may also receive bonus pay for reaching sales goals. Their benefits may include paid vacations and holidays, health insurance, and a pension plan.

Job Description

Companies advertise to increase their sales. People may buy furniture because they hear radio advertisements about a sale. A family may try a new restaurant advertised in the newspaper. Supermarket shoppers may choose a brand of ice cream they saw advertised on television.

Advertising does two things. It informs buyers about products and prices in the marketplace. It also tries to persuade people to buy. Advertising may focus on quality, price, service, or features. A newspaper ad for the All-Brand Appliance Store may describe the latest-model clothes drier. But it will also try to persuade people to buy the drier, and buy it from All-Brand.

Advertising sales workers speak with potential advertisers and discuss their needs. Workers describe the audience an advertiser will reach. Each station and publication keeps statistics about its audience. An amusement park may be happy to buy a $200 ad on a radio station popular with sixteen- to thirty-four-year-olds. It may not want to spend $200 to reach people over fifty-five. Sales workers try to contact advertisers who will benefit most from their advertising. They use statistics to explain the benefit.

An advertising sales worker discusses display ads with a group of advertisers.

Sales workers discuss other options as well. Radio and television ads can run at various times during the day. The number of people listening varies, as does the price of ads. The more people the advertisement reaches, the more it will cost. For this reason, the price also increases with size. Newspaper and magazine advertisers can choose full-page display ads or two-line classified ads. Most radio and television ads run from fifteen seconds to one minute.

Advertisers may be able to choose where and when their ads run. Radio and television advertisers usually pay for a certain time period. But they often have to pay extra if they want to advertise at an exact time. For example, a store may want to advertise raincoats during the weather forecast on the evening news. Magazine advertisers pay more for their ads to appear on the back cover.

Advertising sales workers help advertisers choose from among the many options. The sales workers may arrange for the ads to be produced. Some sales workers help write radio or television advertisements. They follow up after the ads have run. Sales workers can make more money if advertisers run ads on a regular basis.

Outlook for Jobs

People interested in advertising sales can begin preparing while in high school. Two types of experience can be helpful. Many stores hire high school students to work evenings, on weekends, or during vacation periods. Students may help customers or work at cash registers. This experience can help students develop sales skills.

Students may also find part-time jobs at newspapers or radio stations. They may work as office assistants or messengers. These jobs give students a chance to learn about the business. Students can also speak with people who sell advertising.

Advertising sales workers can advance by moving to larger stations or publications. They may also become advertising sales managers or account executives. Some take jobs with company advertising departments or advertising agencies.

The future is bright for advertising sales workers. Magazines, newspapers, and radio and television stations depend on money from advertising. Also, companies are making more and more consumer goods. They count on advertising to inform and influence buyers. As a result, the number of jobs for advertising sales workers will continue to increase.

For more information on advertising sales workers, write to:

Newspaper Advertising Bureau
1180 Avenue of the Americas, Third Floor
New York, NY 10036
(212) 921–5080

Radio Advertising Bureau
304 Park Avenue South
New York, NY 10010
(212) 254–4800

Television Bureau of Advertising
477 Madison Avenue
New York, NY 10022–5892
(212) 486–1111

Chapter 11
Real Estate Agent

Real estate agents sell houses, apartments, business and professional office buildings, and industrial properties. Most agents specialize in residential, commercial, or industrial properties. Some arrange property rentals as well. Real estate agents usually work for real estate brokers. Brokers own real estate agencies.

Education, Training, and Salary

Real estate agents do not need to meet any educational requirements. However, all agents must have a state real estate license. To receive a license, people must pass a written exam. Most people need a high school education to pass the exam.

The real estate license exam tests knowledge of rules and laws about the sale of real estate. Some training is necessary to prepare for the exam. Many real estate agencies offer training classes. Community and junior colleges also offer real estate courses. Most states require people to have at least thirty hours of classroom instruction before taking the exam.

High school graduates often work while they study for the exam. Many are hired by real estate agencies to work in their offices. These workers learn about real estate sales as they work with experienced agents.

The pay of real estate agents varies widely. New workers without a license are paid about the same as other clerical workers are paid. They earn between $9,000 and $12,000 a year. Licensed agents earn a commission on each sale they make. That means they receive a percentage of the sale price. New full-time agents earn between $19,000 and $21,000. With experience, agents can earn up to $35,000. Some agents earn much more.

Part-time real estate agents do not usually receive benefits. Some brokers provide benefits for full-time employees. Benefits may include paid vacations and holidays, health insurance, and a pension plan. Other agents provide their own benefits.

Job Description

Real Estate Office Worker   Real estate office workers have some general office duties. But they also have certain real estate duties. They may

- Answer telephone calls from people who want information about properties for sale
- Keep records of property sales and rentals
- Type new property listings or enter them into a computer
- Arrange to advertise properties in area newspapers and magazines
- Prepare property sale documents for agents
- Gather lists of potential customers for agents

A couple receives the keys to their new house from the real estate agent.

These duties help workers learn how real estate is sold. They can also develop useful sales skills. This experience may help workers pass the real estate license exam and make them better real estate agents.

Real Estate Agent   Real estate agents help people do two things: buy properties and sell properties. Some people contact an agent when they want to buy a property. So agents need to keep up to date. They study listings of many different properties. By reading real estate papers, they stay informed about market conditions and property values.

Agents try to match people to the right properties. They ask questions to find out exactly what

77

people have in mind. Agents then decide which properties the people may be interested in. They take the people to see the properties. Most people look at many different properties before making a decision.

When a customer decides to buy a property, the agent contacts the seller's agent. The agent tells the seller's agent what price the buyer is offering. If the offer is accepted, the agent works with the customer to complete the sale. Contracts and agreements must be filled out. Most buyers need to borrow money to buy a property. The agent may help the buyer apply for a mortgage.

Real estate agents also sell houses. They may call people who may need to sell their properties. People usually list a property with a certain agent for three to six months. The agent helps the seller decide on a price. Some minor repairs may be suggested by the agent so the property will be more attractive. Then the agent places the property in a central real estate sales listing. That way other agents in the area know the property is for sale.

After agents list a property, they try to find a buyer. Agents get a commission for selling a house. But they also receive a small commission when a house they list is sold by another agent.

Some real estate agents arrange property rentals. They show properties to customers who want to rent apartments, homes, office buildings, or even factories. They describe the properties and the rental costs. Agents write rental agreements and have them signed by the owners and the renters. Some agents also manage rental properties for their owners.

Outlook for Jobs

People interested in a sales career in real estate should begin preparing while in high school. Many stores hire high school students to work evenings, on weekends, or during vacation periods. Students may help customers or work at cash registers. This experience can help students develop their sales skills. Part-time clerical work in an office can also help students get ahead.

Real estate agents can advance as they gain experience. Agents often find that their income increases as they make more contacts in the area. Some agents take another exam to become brokers. Then they can open their own real estate businesses. Other agents specialize in commercial, industrial, or expensive residential properties. Still others become real estate appraisers or property managers.

Real estate is not an easy career to get into. New agents often begin part-time. Changes in the economy can affect real estate sales. Many agents leave the field. But those who work hard can do very well.

Real estate agents can earn a lot of money. And they are a key part of the business community. The outlook for real estate agents is very good. People who become successful real estate agents can look forward to rewarding careers.

For more information on real estate agents, write to:

National Association of Realtors
430 North Michigan Avenue
Chicago, IL 60611
(312) 329–8200

Chapter 12
Getting the Job: Tips for the Reader

Starting Out

Whatever job you decide to go after, you want to do it to the best of your ability. And you can do this only if you have picked a job you enjoy. Be honest with yourself. Begin your job search by understanding your talents and interests.

Rate Your Strengths

Write down a few lines about yourself. Tell what you like and what you dislike. List your favorite subjects at school and your least favorite subjects. Describe what bores you and what interests you most.

Make a chart and list any jobs you have ever had. Include your supervisors' names, your work addresses, and the dates of employment. Now make a list of your hobbies or interests. Also list the schools you have attended and the activities you take part in. This list would include clubs or teams you have joined. If you have done any volunteer work, be sure to list it. Finally, add to your list the names of any awards or prizes you have won.

List Your Job Possibilities

List all the jobs in this book that sound interesting. Look at each job and see if you qualify. If a job you like requires extra training, write that down. Also check the publications in the back of this book. Write down the titles of any books or other materials that will tell you more about the jobs you like.

Look at your job list and your strengths list. See where they match up. Put a star by those jobs that would use your strengths.

Consult Counselors

Talk to a guidance counselor at your school. Ask about jobs that are open in your field of interest. Your state or local employment service can also help you.

82

Looking for Work

When you have settled on the jobs you would like, start looking for openings. Apply for as many jobs as you can. The more jobs you apply for, the better your chance of finding one.

Research   Find out everything you can about jobs you are applying for. Learn about the positions, the employers, and the employers' needs. The more you know, the more impressive you will be in your interview.

Ads   There are two types of newspaper classified ads: *help wanted* and *situation wanted*. A help wanted ad is placed by an employer looking to fill a specific job. It tells you the job title, requirements, salary, company, and whom to

ABBREVIATIONS

People who place classified ads often use abbreviations. They want to make their ad as short as possible. Read the classified ad section in your newspaper to become familiar with abbreviations. Here is a short list to help you now:

excel.	excellent	f.t.	
bnfts.	benefits	or f/t	full-time
exp.	experience	emp.	employment
p.t.		gd.	good
or p/t	part-time	refs.	references
h.s.	high school	ext.	extension
grad.	graduate	req.	required
w.	with	sal.	salary
avail.	available	pfd.	preferred
hr.	hour	wk.	week

contact. You may also see a blind ad, one that does not name the employer. Answer the ad by letter or by phone, as directed in the ad. Follow up within two weeks with another phone call or letter if you have not heard from the employer.

A person looking for work can place a situation wanted ad. This ad tells the kind of work the person is looking for and why he or she qualifies. It also tells when he or she could start working.

Networking   Networking is letting everyone know what jobs you are looking for. Talk to people in your field of interest. Some good leads on jobs can be found this way. Friends and relatives might also be able to help. Follow up on what you learn with a phone call or letter.

Employment Services   Check with your school's placement service for job openings. State and local employment services often have job listings.

Civil Service   Federal, state, and local governments offer many jobs. Find the civil service office near you and ask about openings. See the feature on the next page. It explains more about civil service jobs.

Unions   Find out about labor unions that may be involved with jobs in your field. Check with union locals in your town; you can find phone numbers in the phone book.

Temporary Employment   Working on a temporary basis can lead to other jobs or to part-time or full-time work. Seasonal work is available for many jobs.

Federal and state governments employ several million workers. In order to get a government job, you must first check with the Federal Job Information Center or a state department of personnel office. Look for an announcement concerning the type of job that interests you. The announcement describes the job. It also lists the education and experience that you will need to qualify for the job.

Once you know about a government job opening, you must fill out an application to take a civil service test. If your application is approved, you must then take and pass the exam. Exams are usually written, but may also be oral. Some exams include essays or performance tests. All exams are tailored to fit a specific job. An exam may cover such items as English usage, reasoning, or clerical or mechanical skills.

Applying in Person

Applying to an employer in person can be a good idea. Call for an appointment. Tell the employer that you would like to have an interview. Some may ask that you send a letter or résumé first.

Sending Letters

Writing letters can also be a good way to ask about jobs. Typed letters are preferred, but neat, handwritten letters are acceptable. Check the Yellow Pages or industry magazines at the public library for addresses. The librarian can help you. Address letters to a company's personnel or human resources department. Send your résumé with the letter. Keep copies of all letters. Follow up in a couple of weeks with another letter.

Résumé

A résumé is a useful one-page outline of information about you. It introduces you to a possible future employer. A résumé should be based on your strengths list. It sums up your education, work history, and skills.

You will enclose your résumé in letters you write to future employers. You also will take it with you to give to your interviewer. Look at the sample résumé on page 87 to see how a typical résumé looks.

Always put your full name, address, and phone number at the top of the résumé. Type the résumé, if possible, or write it by hand neatly. Then state your objective or the job you are applying for. Put down any experience that shows you are a good worker. Volunteer work and part-time jobs tell an employer that you are willing to help out and work hard. Put down your most recent job first.

Finally, include information about your education. You can also list any special skills, awards, or honors you have received.

Writing Letters

When you send your résumé in the mail, always attach a cover letter. Write a short letter, no more than three or four paragraphs. It should come right to the point and lead the employer to your résumé.

Explain what job you are interested in. Include a short listing of your qualifications. Your letter should catch the employer's interest. That way the employer will want to turn to your résumé. See the sample on page 88.

Résumé

Amanda L. Samuels
6022 South Titus Avenue
Maryville, OH 44776
(614) 555–6678

Objective: To be a sales worker at a clothing store.

Experience
1990   Worked as cashier in Ayers
            Department Store during summer
            vacation.

1989   Worked in fast-food restaurant part-
            time.

Training
Taking fashion-design course at Valley
Community College.

Education
1990   Graduated Lincoln High School.

References available on request.

November 1, 1991
Amanda L. Samuels
6022 South Titus Avenue
Maryville, OH 44776

Manager
Boutique Orleans
Center Square
Buckton

Dear Manager,

I am answering your advertisement for a salesperson that appeared in the *Post Gazette* on October 30.

I am taking a fashion design course at Valley Community College. My work at Ayers Department Store included both sales and cashier work.

I am enclosing my résumé to give you more information about my background. I look forward to hearing from you at your earliest convenience.

Thank you for your time.

Sincerely,

Amanda L. Samuels

enclosure

Completing the Application Form

You may have to fill out an application form when applying for a job. (See the sample on pages 90 and 91.) This form asks for your education, experience, work history, and other information.

The employer may mail an application form to you ahead of time. Or, you may be asked to fill out the form when you come for the interview.

Follow the instructions carefully. Print or type information neatly. Neatness tells the employer that you care about your work. It also shows you can organize information and think clearly.

Have all information with you when you arrive. You will need your Social Security number. You may need to list your past jobs. You will have to give the dates you worked, addresses, and phone numbers.

List your most recent jobs first, as you do on your résumé.

However, do not answer any question that you feel invades your privacy. Laws prevent an employer from asking about certain things. These things include race, religion, national origin, age, and marital status. Questions about your family situation, property, car, or arrest record are also not allowed.

The Interview

The way you act in a job interview will tell the employer a lot about you. It can be the biggest single factor that helps an employer decide whether to hire you. An interview is very important. Therefore, you should prepare yourself to make a good impression.

APPLICATION FOR EMPLOYMENT

(Please print or type your answers)

PERSONAL INFORMATION   Date _____

Name _____ Social Security Number _____/ _____/ _____

Address _____
           Street and Number   City   State   Zip Code

Telephone number (_____) _____ – _____ (_____) _____ – _____
                              day   evening

Job applied for _____ Salary expected $ _____ per _____

How did you learn of this position? _____

Do you want to work _____ Full time or _____ Part time?

Specify preferred days and hours if you answered part time _____

Have you worked for us before? _____ If yes, when? _____

On what date will you be able to start work? _____

Have you ever been convicted of a crime, excluding misdemeanors and summary offenses?

_____ No   _____ Yes

If yes, describe in full _____

Whom should we notify in case of emergency?

Name _____ Relationship _____

Address _____
           Street and number   City   State   Zip Code

Telephone number (_____) _____ – _____ (_____) _____ – _____
                              day   evening

EDUCATION

Type of School	Name and Address	Years Attended	Graduated	Course or Major
High School			Yes No	
College			Yes No	
Post-graduate			Yes No	
Business or Trade			Yes No	
Military or other			Yes No	

WORK EXPERIENCE (List in order, beginning with most recent job)

Dates		Employer's Name and Address	Rate of Pay Start/Finish	Position Held	Reason for Leaving
From	To				

ACTIVITIES AND HONORS (List any academic, extracurricular, civic, or other achievements you consider significant.)

_____

_____

PERSONAL REFERENCES
_____

Name and Occupation   Address   Phone Number

_____

_____

_____

PLEASE READ THE FOLLOWING STATEMENTS CAREFULLY AND SIGN BELOW:

The information that I have provided on this application is accurate to the best of my knowledge and is subject to validation. I authorize the schools, persons, current employer, and other organizations or employers named in this application to provide any relevant information that may be required to arrive at an employment decision.

_____   _____
Applicant's Signature   Date

Before you go to the interview, prepare what you will say. Think of why you want the job, your experience, and why you qualify. Learn as much about the job and the company as possible. You can do this through ads, brochures, employees, or your library. This will show that you are interested in the company's needs.

Make a list of questions you have. And try to guess what the interviewer will ask. You may ask if you can work overtime or if you can take courses for more training or education. Bring in any certificates or licenses you may need to show.

Dress neatly and appropriately for the interview. Make sure you know exactly where the interview will take place so you will be on time. Allow extra time to get there in case you are delayed by traffic or for some other reason.

Following Up

After the interview, thank the interviewer for his or her time and shake hands. If the job appeals to you, tell the person that you are interested.

When you get back home, send a letter thanking the interviewer for his or her time. Repeat things that were discussed in the interview. Keep a copy of it and start a file for all future letters.

Think about how you acted in the interview. Did you ask the right questions? Were your answers right? Did you feel you should have done something differently? If so, make notes so you can do better the next time.

If you do not hear from the company in two weeks, write a letter. Tell the interviewer you are still interested in the job. You can also phone to follow up.

Know Your Rights: What Is the Law?

Federal   Under federal law, employers cannot discriminate on the basis of race, religion, sex, national origin, ancestry, or age. People aged forty to seventy are specifically protected against age discrimination. Handicapped workers also are protected. Of course, these laws protect only workers who do their jobs. Employers need not hire workers who are unqualified. And they are free to fire workers who do not perform.

State   Many states have laws against discrimination based on age, handicap, or membership in armed services reserves. Laws differ from state to state. In some states, there can be no enforced retirement age. And some protect people suffering from AIDS.

Applications   When filling out applications, you do not have to answer questions that may invade your privacy. Questions about whether you are married, have children, own property or a car do not have to be answered. Nor do you have to answer questions about an arrest record. An employer may ask, however, if you have ever been convicted of a crime.

At Work   It is against the law for employers to discriminate against workers when setting hours, workplace conditions, salary, hirings, layoffs, firings, or promotions. And no employer can treat a worker unfairly if he or she has filed a discrimination suit or taken other legal action.

Read Your Contract   Read any work contract you are given. Do not sign it until you understand and agree to everything in it. Ask questions if you have them. If you have used an employment agency, find out about fees before you sign a contract. Some agencies will charge you a fee for finding a job. Others charge the employer.

When Discrimination Occurs: What You Can Do

Government Help Call the Equal Employment Opportunity Commission or the state civil rights commission if you feel you've been discriminated against. If they think you have been unfairly treated, they may take legal action. If you have been unfairly denied a job, you may get it. If you have been unfairly fired, you may get your job back and receive pay that is owed you. Any mention of the actions taken against you may be removed from your work records. To file a lawsuit, you will need a lawyer.

Private Help Private organizations such as the American Civil Liberties Union (ACLU) and the National Association for the Advancement of Colored People (NAACP) fight against discrimination. They can give you advice.

94

Sources

General Career Information

Abrams, Kathleen S. *Guide to Careers Without College.* New York: Franklin Watts, 1988.

Career Information Center, 4th ed., 13 vols. Mission Hills, Calif.: Glencoe/Macmillan, 1990.

Dubrovin, Vivian. *Guide to Alternative Education and Training.* New York: Franklin Watts, 1988.

Hopke, William E., editor in chief. *The Encyclopedia of Career and Vocational Guidance*, 7th ed., 3 vols. Chicago: Ferguson, 1987.

Littrell, J. J. *From School to Work.* South Holland, Ill.: Goodheart-Willcox, 1984.

Occupational Outlook Handbook. Washington, D.C.: U.S. Government Printing Office, revised biennially.

Perry, Robert L. *Guide to Self-Employment.* New York: Franklin Watts, 1989.

Primm, E. Russell III, editor in chief. *Career Discovery Encyclopedia,* 6 vols. Chicago: Ferguson, 1990.

Sales and Distribution Careers

Evans, Marilyn. *Opportunities in Real Estate.* Skokie, Ill.: VGM Career Horizons, 1983.

Fry, Ronald W. *Marketing and Sales Career Directory.* Hawthorne, N.J.: Career Press, 1988.

Pattis, S. William. *Opportunities in Advertising.* Lincolnwood, Ill.: National Textbook Company, 1984.

Rosenthal, David W., and Michael A. Powell. *Careers in Marketing.* Englewood Cliffs, N.J.: Prentice-Hall, 1984.

Shinn, George. *Introduction to Professional Selling.* New York: Gregg/McGraw-Hill, 1982.

Index